IMPROVISING
BOOGIE-WOOGIE

Volume Three

Southern House Publishing

Copyright © 2021 Southern House Publishing

All rights reserved.
No part of this book may be reproduced in any form
by electronic, mechanical or other means
without prior permission from the publisher.

ISBN: 978-1-9196118-2-2

tylermusic.co.uk

CONTENTS

Introduction	1 - 2
Key Points	3 - 6
Left-Hand Patterns 1	7 - 12
Using Thirds	13 - 30
Creating Riffs (Thirds)	31 - 33
Left-Hand Patterns 2	34 - 39
Using Sixths	40 - 50
Blues And Pentatonics	51 - 61
Scales In Boogie	62 - 72
Twiddly Boogie Riffs	73 - 97
Creating Riffs	98 - 108
Changing Position	109 - 120
16/32 Bar Progressions	121 - 132
24-Bar Progressions	133 - 135
Practice Suggestions	136 - 136
Downloadable Audio	137 - 137

An Introduction

Welcome to volume three of Improvising boogie-woogie. Boogie-woogie is a fantastic and addictive style of piano that although no-longer mainstream, it perseveres within its own niche market and shows no signs of dying out. It's still popular today among those with (dare I say it) good taste in music. So congratulate yourself for being such a person, us fellow boogie people salute you.

Being volume three in the series it's a fair assumption that you are already familiar with the previous volumes. Here we take things a little further and along with a number of new left-hand patterns to work on. This volume concentrates primarily on the improvising side of things, looking at how the music is created. Covering aspects like scales, thirds and sixths it moves onto how to use them to create your own riffs, which includes looking at how to alter existing music. To end with, it also takes a look at some more complex, longer chord progressions.

The difficulty level varies within, some things are easier, others are quite tricky, so although I don't like labels you could say it's at an intermediate level, perhaps, you can judge for yourselves. But if you are using this volume then you're probably past the complete beginner level and would have already worked through the previous volumes anyway.

Remember, the book is part of a series and must be looked upon as such, individually it is quite incomplete with all volumes required to make up the whole picture. Each volume covers different aspects with new information and examples of increasing difficulty as it progresses, so to continue learning more, don't forget the preceding volumes.

Right then, if you've read all of that I'll simply finish by saying that I hope you find the book helpful, but above all else... just enjoy playing your boogie-woogie, it is after-all what it's all about.

Key Points

Before you step further into the book, there are a couple of points to go over first, just to clarify a few things that will continue on throughout the series.

The Shuffle Feel Notation

Boogie-woogie tends to be played with a shuffle feel, or alternatively you could refer to it as a triplet feel. The music throughout the book is played with such a shuffle feel, so it's important to get this right before moving any further and to understand how it will be notated.

The music has a kind of long/short jumping sound that gives it the shuffle feel. This is created because each beat has two notes, the first being twice as long as the second. This is created by splitting each beat into three (triplets) with the first having the value of two triplets and the second one triplet.

Triplet Shuffle Feel

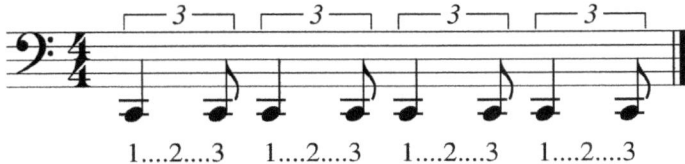

Now... for practical reasons, music with a shuffle feel is rarely written using actual triplets like above, instead it's fairly common practice to use straight quavers (8th notes) instead. This is accompanied by a sign (like the one below) telling you that the eighth notes actually denote a triplet feel instead, with the first two note longer than the second.

Triplet Feel Sign

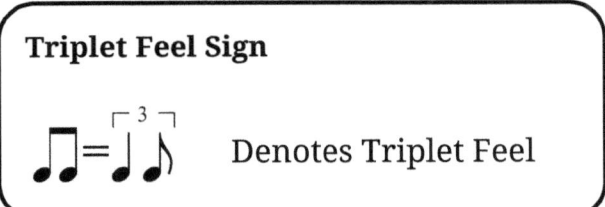

Denotes Triplet Feel

Example Of Notation Using Eighths

You can see below the true value of the eighth notes with how the triplets line up with the straight eighth notes.

This idea might be new to you, or you might have plenty of experience with it already, either way it's simple enough and soon becomes second nature. At times triplets will still be shown it just depends on if they are required or not, but for the majority of the time the book will have the shuffle feel notated as straight eighths.

Putting This Into Context

So let's put this into context with an actual boogie-woogie left-hand pattern. First we have a chopping type pattern notated using triplets (technically correct).

Triplet Notation (Technically Correct)

Next we have the same pattern notated as straight quavers (eighth notes) with the symbol denoting the true timing value of the notes.

Eighth-Note Notation

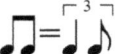

IMPORTANT

Always remember that the eighth notes *are not* eighth notes, they are played as triplets. The first note being long (two triplets value) the second note shorter (one triplet value).

This form of notation has been chosen for the book as it seems to have become the standard way of notating boogie and blues music. It's easier on the eye and once the shuffle feel has been practised for a time, it eventually becomes second nature, and you won't even think twice about it.

The Chord Symbols

The chord symbols in the examples are not always indicative of the specific chords within that bar, like '**D13**' or '**D6**' but rather simply shows the general chord in order to show the position within the chord progression. This is because, due to the nature of the music the left-hand doesn't always match specifically with the right-hand. You can be moving between all manner of chords within a short space, making it less than practical to be overly specific. Also, with its improvisational nature, it's best to think of the general chord of each bar with regard to the chord progression. Within a bar that is '**F**' for example, you are open to using many versions of that basic chord.

Key Choices

For the most part the key of choice used here shouldn't surprise anyone. For ease of understanding and explanation the key of '**C**' is an obvious and sensible choice, as it's easier to follow and absorb the information this way rather than use a key with five sharps. The first volume in the series will stay within this one key, although it does have a section that discusses playing in different keys. Of course, ultimately we don't only want to play in '**C**', so to help push things on further, the following two volumes include examples in other keys. Although for obvious reasons we don't have room to cover everything, but some of the more common keys are used to encourage their use.

Fingering Options

Fingering numbers haven't been included here, it wouldn't be practical to do so and besides, anyone here will have some degree of understanding on how to approach the keyboard when given something new to play. There is no all knowing governing body telling us how we should be playing boogie-woogie and the likes of Ammons or Yancy would have just played as came natural to them. If you find a comfortable way to play, and it works well for you then it's probably right, if you are struggling then maybe re-think it. There are basic rules approaching fingering that tend to work well, but... With the nature of boogie it's best not to limit yourself to a set pattern that may not always be optimal in every circumstance, try to be open and fluid.

Tempo

The speed at which you play the music is (to a degree) up to you. Boogie-woogie might be anything between 100–170 bpm or maybe more (although it can become too fast if you ask me). But, I've stayed away from being too specific regarding speed as this can be off-putting to some and might cause them to try to play something faster than they are ready to. You can match the tempo of the audio examples if you wish, but starting off slower is a good general rule that should be followed. If you listen to boogie-woogie then you will know the kind of tempo that works, but don't rush to play fast. Speed comes as a by-product of accuracy, it comes with time so start at a tempo you can handle and gradually increase it as you improve, don't rush it, just let it happen naturally.

Left-Hand Pattern 1

Before we get started on the improvisation side of things, let's get warmed up with this great little left-hand pattern. Based around the root, third, fifth and sixth, it's unusual in that it also includes the fourth as a stepping stone up to the fifth.

12-bar Practice Example

1 🔊 AUDIO

A couple of variations are shown below, the differences are minor, so play whichever version you prefer. Personally I use either the top one or variation two.

Variation. 1

Variation. 2

Boogie On Fourth

Using Thirds

It's quite common to hear riffs and even whole passages created using thirds. Often they are mixed with other ideas, but at times they can be used solely on their own, creating a riff or a run down the keyboard using nothing but thirds. Learning them all, having them memorised and practised sufficiently to recall when playing without thought is really useful for improvising.

Third Interval

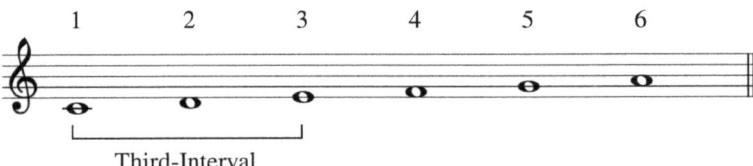

As shown in the diagram above, a third is two notes that are three intervals apart. The second note is two steps (through the scale) higher than the first. This applies to all positions throughout the scale.

Third Interval Examples

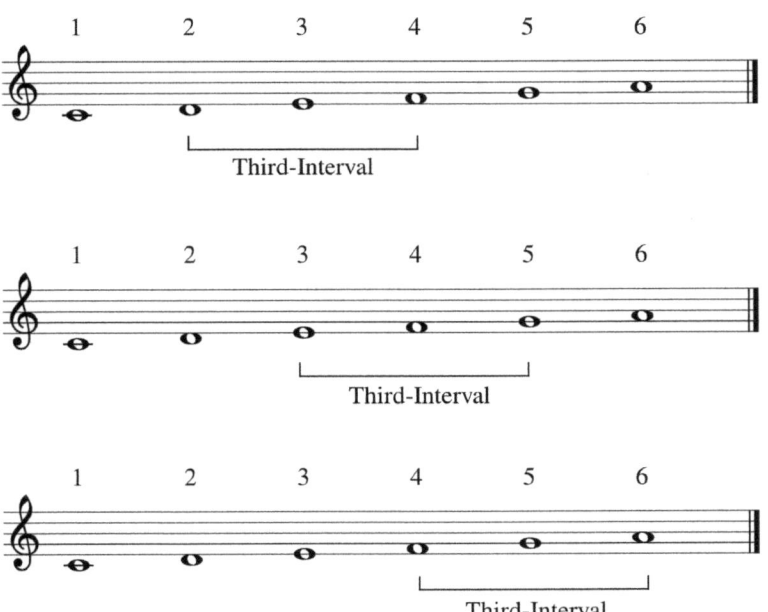

Let's start by looking at the thirds created from the major scale. I will point out straight away that this is very limiting and not entirely suited for our purpose (although usable at times) so afterwards we will move on to add some more interesting options to it.

Thirds Built On 'C' Major

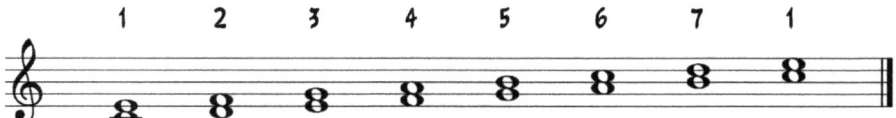

Here we have the thirds built from the major scale, each one is built upon the intervals of the scale. They're easy to remember as essentially it's just the major scale, but with an extra note added above. You can see three more examples of this built upon the **'F'**, **'G'** and **'D'** major scales below.

Thirds Built In Key Of 'F'

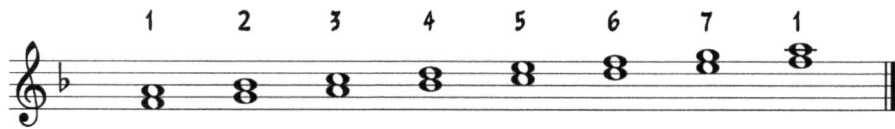

Thirds Built In Key Of 'G'

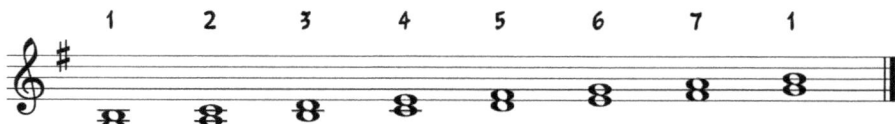

Thirds Built In Key Of 'D'

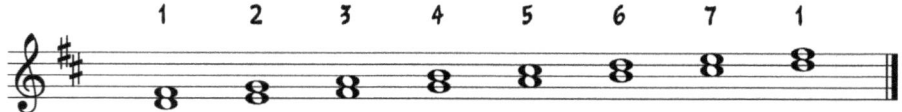

If you know your major scales then it's easy to work out the thirds for whatever key you are in, even if it's a key you haven't really been working with.

So with the basics over, let's put them into context and see how they work within boogie-woogie. You'll see how the ones used here fit perfectly, but you may notice two things. It lacks that blues sound, it's too upright and... well, major. Also, that we have stayed away from certain thirds, two in particular as they contain the major-seventh which clashes somewhat, so this needs altering for them to be more useable.

Example 12-bar (Using Only Major Thirds)

Additional Thirds

So having looked at the basic thirds built upon the major scale, we have seen that being entirely from the major scale they lacked something of the blues element that we require here. Step in the flat/dominant seventh.

Thirds With Flat-Seventh (Key Of 'C')

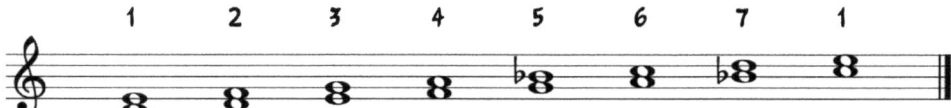

For the most part we have the same scale, except we are replacing the major-seventh with the flat/dominant seventh. This note is from the minor pentatonic, minor blues scale and Mixolydian mode. All of these are more suitable for boogie-woogie duty than the good old major scale.

Thirds With Flat-Seventh (Key Of 'F')

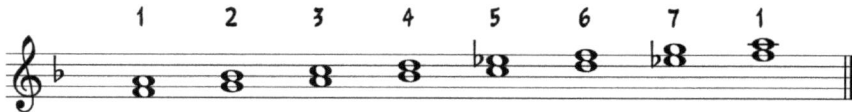

Thirds With Flat-Seventh (Key Of 'G')

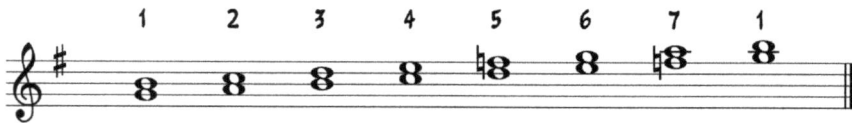

Thirds With Flat-Seventh (Key Of 'D')

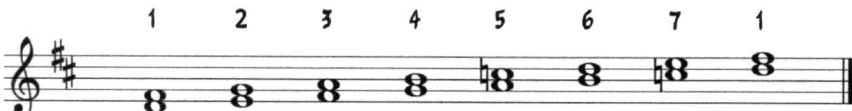

Again these are easy to work out if you already know the major scales and in turn the major-third intervals. All you need to do is to remember to flatten the seventh.

Additional Minor-Third

Here we will add the minor-third to the mix, which creates more interest again, although it is quite dissonant (more so than the seventh) so requires careful use.

Thirds With Minor-Third (Key Of 'C')

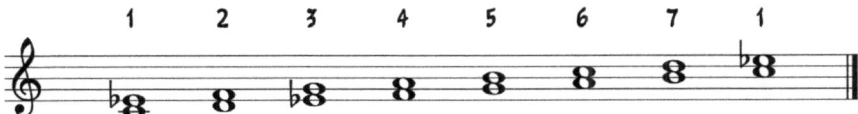

The minor-third is found within the minor pentatonic, minor blues scale and the major blues scales, so it can be used to good effect.

Thirds With Minor-Third (Key Of 'F')

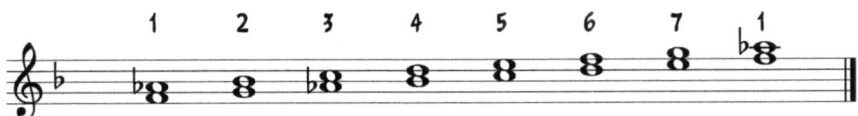

Thirds With Minor-Third (Key Of 'G')

A run of thirds using the minor-third doesn't sound very good in a blues context (have a play around with it and see) but it works very well when used in conjunction with the major third. Switching between the major and minor thirds is a common thing in boogie. The run of thirds shown above do work well however when you combine them with the flat-seventh instead of the major.

Diminished Thirds (Key Of 'C')

I'm referring to this addition as 'diminished' as the two notes in question can be found within a diminished scale and would create a diminished chord if added to the root note. We are referring to the flat-third and flat-fifth.

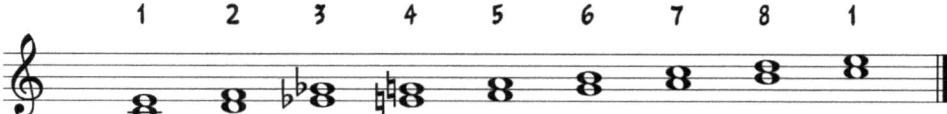

The two notes above have an addition as opposed to altering any of the existing notes in the scale. Both the flat-third and flat-fifth can be found within the minor-blues scale. The third and fifth still remain though, as they work very nicely with the flat-third and flat-fifth. The switching back and forth is a common blues thing, the dissonant sound of the flat-third/fifth resolving back to the major sound.

Diminished Thirds (Key Of 'F')

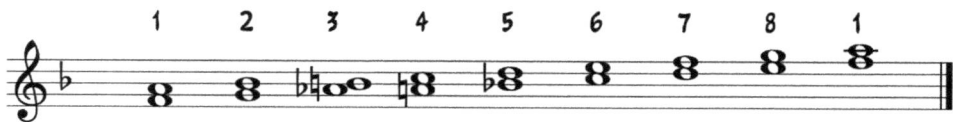

Diminished Thirds (Key Of 'G')

The following pages have the thirds shown in every key. Learning/practising them like this may be tiresome, but drilling them into your subconscious will help a great deal when improvising.

Note

In order to make them work better musically, they have been combined in two different combinations. The diminished with the seventh and the minor-third with the flat-seventh.

Thirds Practice 1

Thirds With Diminished And Flat-Seventh   (A To D)

A

B♭

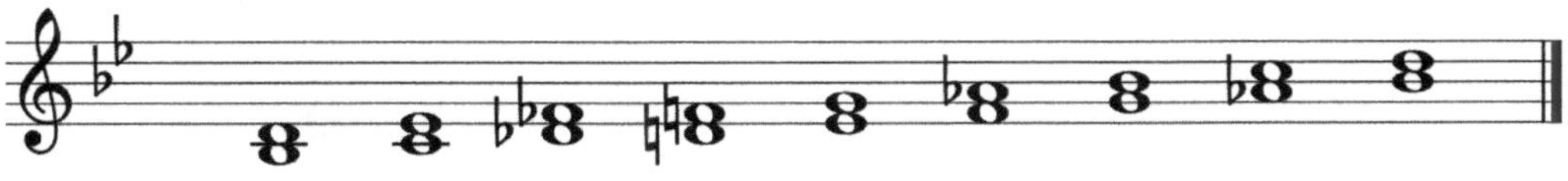

B

C

D♭

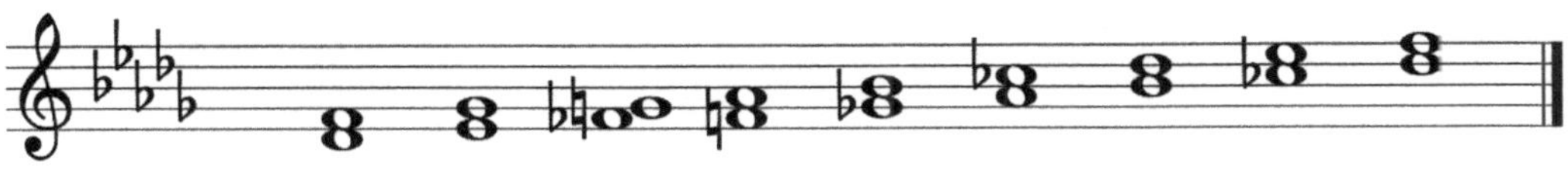

D

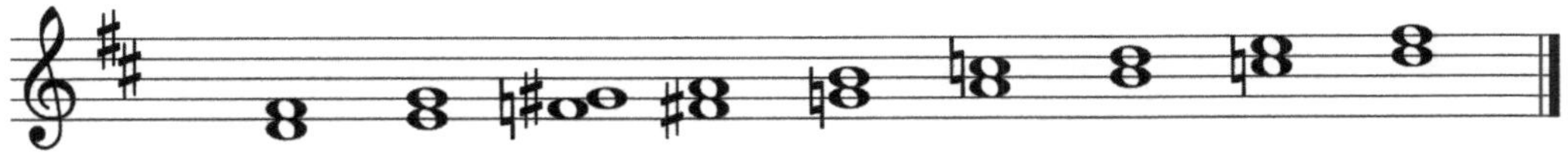

Thirds With Diminished And Flat-Seventh   (E♭ To A♭)

E♭

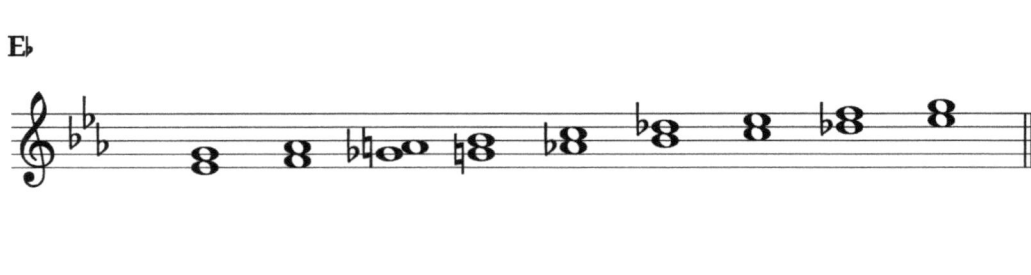

E

F

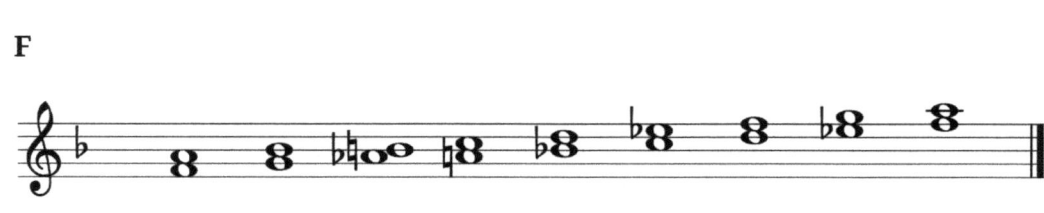

G♭

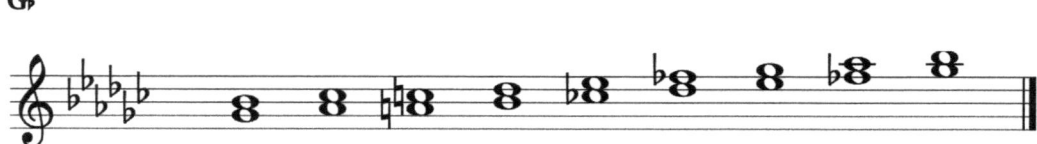

G

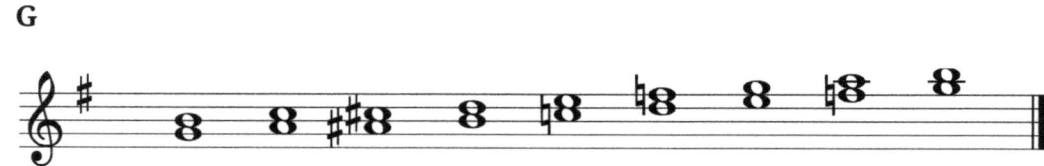

A♭

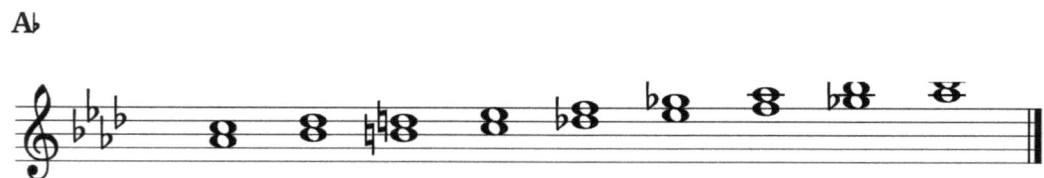

Thirds Practice 2

Thirds With Minor-Third and Flat-Seventh   (A To D)

A

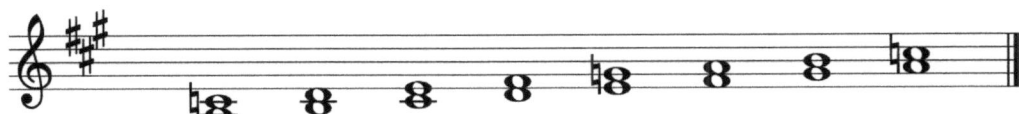

B♭

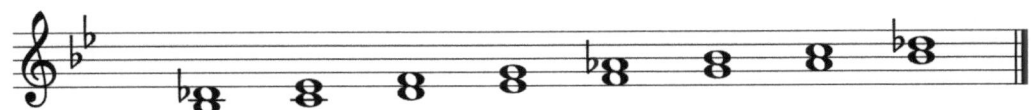

B

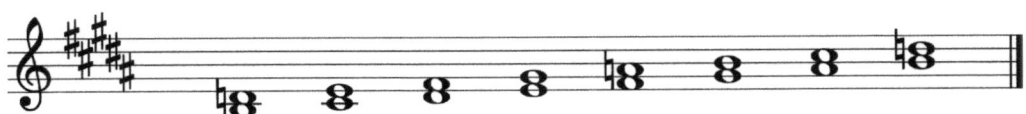

C

D♭

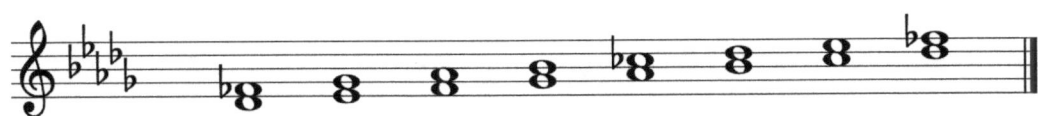

D

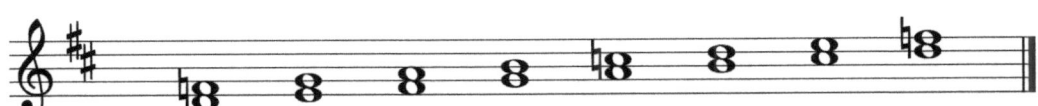

Thirds With Minor-Third and Flat-Seventh   (E♭ To A♭)

E♭

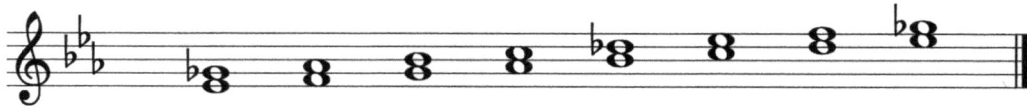

E

F

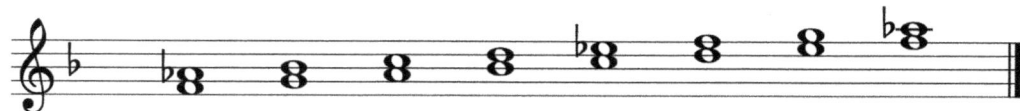

G♭

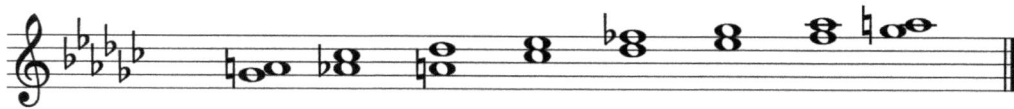

G

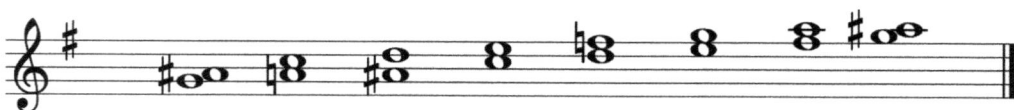

A♭

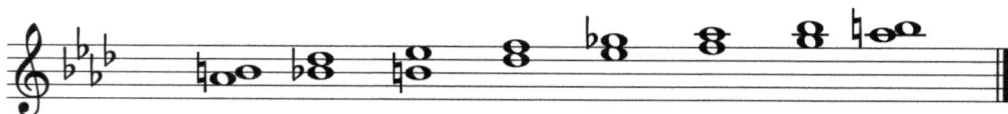

Runs With Thirds

One thing you can do with thirds is incorporate them into a run down the keyboard (Or alternatively, up the keyboard). This can be done in many ways, either completely straight (as shown below) or with a more up and down random movement even mixed in with other ideas/riffs.

1.

Built off the major scale with no alterations.

2.

Additional flat-third and flat-fifth.

3.

Using flat-third and flat-seventh.

4.

Using triplets timing.

5.

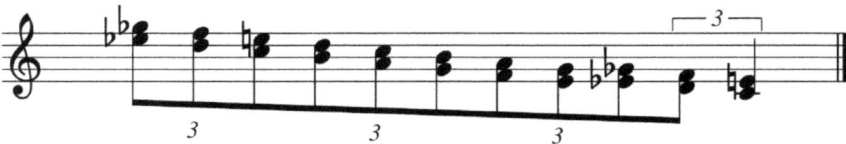

6.

Running downwards with additional upwards movement.

7.

A variation with a similar movement pattern.

8.

Repeating each third (played twice each).

9.

Varying the timing with some notes held longer, here with the third being tied between bars.

There are more riffs with thirds than you can sensibly put in any book, but we can take a look at some ideas that you can make use of, which will hopefully lead you to create ideas of your own.

1.

A mix of long and short notes.

2.

Add some triplets.

3.

You don't have to only use thirds, so mix them in with both chords or single note parts.

4.

Introduce tremolos on the longer notes. It's a great sound and also gives you a breath whilst playing.

5.

A common form of pattern sees you use a series of thirds that alternate with a single lower note below them.

6.

7.

Or... below has you using thirds in a more repetitive way.

8.

9.

10.

11.

Runaway Boogie

Creating Riffs From Thirds

The aim of this book is to help in improvising, so with this in mind, now would be a good time to have a play around with making riffs with thirds. This isn't meant to be a definitive list, but rather to prompt you into experimenting yourself and seeing what works and what doesn't, this is how we learn, trying things out for ourselves.

Keeping within '**C**' for simplicity we are going to walk through an improvisation in slow motion. Below we have some options to choose from again. You can start from anywhere, but music often starts within its chord tones, so that's a good place to begin.

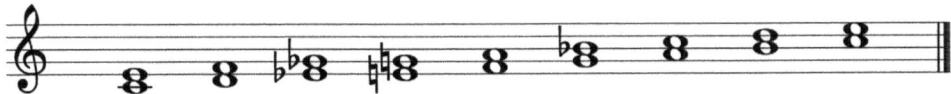

So with this in mind, choose a starting point. Below we are using the chord tones (root and third).

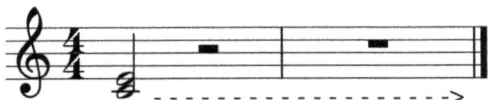

So now what...

Consider These Points

- Are you moving up or down?
- Jumping to another position?
- Moving slowly or fast?
- Using triplets?
- Using a tremolo or alternating pattern?

If you aren't sure where you want the music to go, just pick something or somewhere randomly, continue on and see where it takes you. Sometimes an improvisation can be average and another time it can spark something great. Naturally, like anything it gets better with practice, so it doesn't matter where it leads, the thing to do is just play.

So this is where we are starting...

We could move slowly and steady like this...

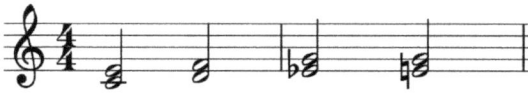

Or a little quicker...

If we choose the latter, what to play? We have no plan, so using some thirds close to the starting point we alternate up and down between them, simple enough.

Now what? There's still no plan, so we repeat the pattern for a moment before moving downwards, safely back to the chord tones we originally began with.

Alternatively, from this same starting point you might have felt like playing triplets instead.

Keeping it simple we move up again from the starting point.

What next? We could just play continuous triplets with the same notes over the whole bar.

Or relax the music at the end by slowing it down slightly with the longer note, and moving back to where we began with.

> This is just to prompt you into playing around with improvising, now experiment with as many ideas as you can come up with. Some will be better than others, but that is how we learn.

Left-Hand Pattern 2

This left-hand pattern is very much like a walking bass-line except that it's cut short and steps back on itself. Although it feels similar to play, it's probably a fair bit easier.

12-bar Practice Example

On bars nine and ten of a twelve-bar, you could always swap out this pattern for a simple alternating octave using the chord root note. It's optional of course, but you could throw it in sometimes to break up the monotony.

Variation

The next song example uses this variation throughout. You could just use the main pattern if you wish, or switch it about. It's in '**G**' and continues with the thirds along with some single note twiddly bits in triplets, which we will have a good look at later on.

Boogie The Third

Using Sixths

As well as using thirds, it's a good idea to get used to playing around with sixths as well, as these intervals are used fairly often with the right-hand.

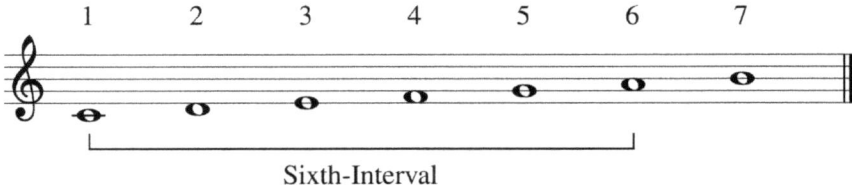

As shown in the diagram above, a sixth is two notes that are six intervals apart. The second note is five steps (through the scale) higher than the first.

Relationship To Thirds

Something you may or may not have noticed is that a sixth has a lot in common with a third, in-fact they use exactly the same notes, but they have been inverted/swapped around.

Sixth

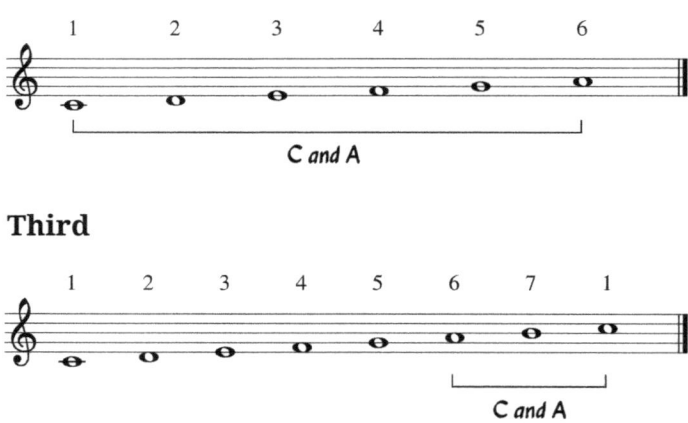

Third

The relationship between them doesn't have a huge significance here, but it does help understand and learn them. Once you know the thirds off by heart then it's easier to get your head around the sixths, as you can see if it's the correct note or not, as it has to match up to a third interval. Any general knowledge always helps with working things out.

Sixth Options In 'C'

Here we have sixths you might use. You can see that it's been altered from the standard major scale as per-usual. We've omitted the major-seventh in favour of the flat/dominant seventh, and included the flat-third and flat-fifth, otherwise it's from a '**C**' major scale.

Example Patterns

So that's a few ideas that you can use with sixths. Unlike thirds, they aren't quite as flexible, by this I mean that they are best used in-conjunction with other ideas, as steps within something larger, it's difficult to create much using only sixths alone. So now we have to put it into some real life context and experiment with different ways of using these within an actual boogie-woogie piece. You can use the next example pieces to practice using the sixth interval.

Boogie On The Six

Six Times Boogie

The Scales Behind The Music

The many riffs, licks, and melody lines you hear in boogie-woogie are obviously made up of notes, but being a blues based style, they tend to come from a specific source, or at least the majority of the time.

Boogie-woogie piano is a form of blues or at least a specific sub-set of it, and as such it's created from the same material, being the major/minor blues scales. These are modified pentatonic scales and are often considered to not even be real by traditional music theory, but their use over all these years tends to tell a different story.

Interesting Note

The major-blues scale is strangely not as well known as the minor-blues, which is often referred to as the '*blues scale*' as if there is only one. But it's a very important scale to know for boogie-woogie.

Reasons To Learn The Blues Scale

- Understanding how various riffs and melodies are created.

- Aid in transposing the music into different keys.

- Help in creating/improvising your own music.

The thought of scales can turn some people off, and I can understand that, but if you feel that way, please persevere. They are very important to know if you want to go beyond sheet-music and improvise your own boogie-woogie (and that's where the real fun is).

Bear in mind that although they are important, there's no need to punish yourself with endless monotonous practice, it's this that can put people off (although if it doesn't, by all means practise as much as you want). I'd suggest instead to practice a little on a regular basis (every day if you can) but just for a little while, so as not to drive you insane. Keep doing this and in time it will add up and make a huge difference to your knowledge and skills.

- **Understanding how riffs are created**

With knowledge of the scales that are used you will be able to understand how the different pattern/riffs within songs that you learn (from sheet music or by ear) were created. This will help you learn the music itself, as once you know that a particular part or run down the keyboard uses a specific set of notes from a scale, it then becomes easier to learn, play and even remember.

- **Aid in transposing the music into different keys**

Knowing the scales will also allow you to dissect a pattern/riff and think of it in terms of its origin within a scale (i.e. the root, third, or fifth etc.) Once you can do that, when you want to play the same thing in a different key you will then know which scale intervals it was created from, which in turn allows you to re-create it in another key. This really saves a lot of time, thought and effort.

- **Help in creating/improvising your own music**

If you are creating your own boogie-woogie music, knowing the scales will help endlessly in being able to improvise new parts, or even modify old ones that you already know. Improvisation isn't magic, it's just using a wealth of stored/practised knowledge that you have picked up and then implementing it at will. Sometimes it isn't perfect, sometimes you get something great, but it's all based on what you have picked up over time.

First off we need to have a quick look at the scales in question (if you already know them then that's great). On the following pages we have both the pentatonic and the blues scales (basically a modified pentatonic) shown in every key. This is followed by a few suggestions on how you might practise them, and then we look at how you can use them.

The Pentatonic Scales

First we have the pentatonic scales, they consist of five notes (hence the 'pent' part of the name). This won't be the main focus here as they're related to the blues scales (being what the blues scales are built from). There is only one note between them, but that note does make a difference, so when the pentatonic is used (or that extra note is omitted) you do have a different sound, so it's useful to remember. And of course the scale is used in other styles as well.

Major-Pentatonic

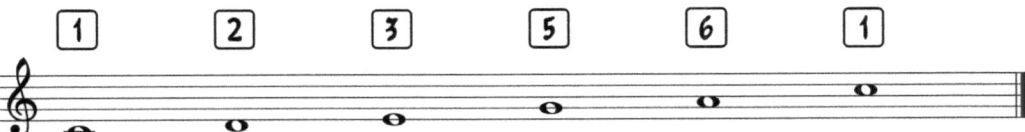

The major-pentatonic is created from the following...

- Root
- Second
- Third
- Fifth
- Sixth

Minor-Pentatonic

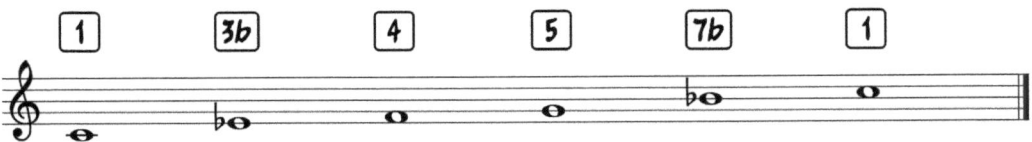

The minor-pentatonic is created from the following...

- Root
- Flat-Third
- Fourth
- Fifth
- Flat-Seventh

The Blues Scales

The blues scales are essentially the pentatonic scales with an additional note. This might not sound like a major difference but the extra note (the so called 'blue notes') goes a long way to create some of the magic, it's surprising how much difference one note actually makes. The major-blues scale is not as well known (shockingly even unheard of by many experienced players) but it certainly does exist and is quite important to know.

Major-Blues

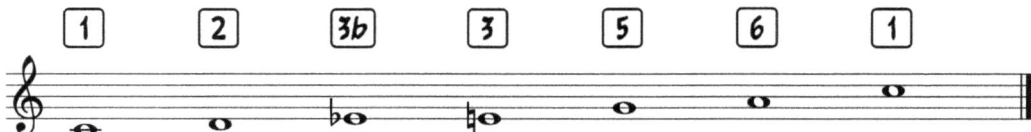

The major-blues scale is created from the following...

- Root
- Second
- Flat-Third
- Third
- Fifth
- Sixth

Minor-Blues

The minor-blues scale is created from the following...

- Root
- Flat-Third
- Fourth
- Flat-Fifth
- Fifth
- Flat-Seventh

Major-Blues Scales

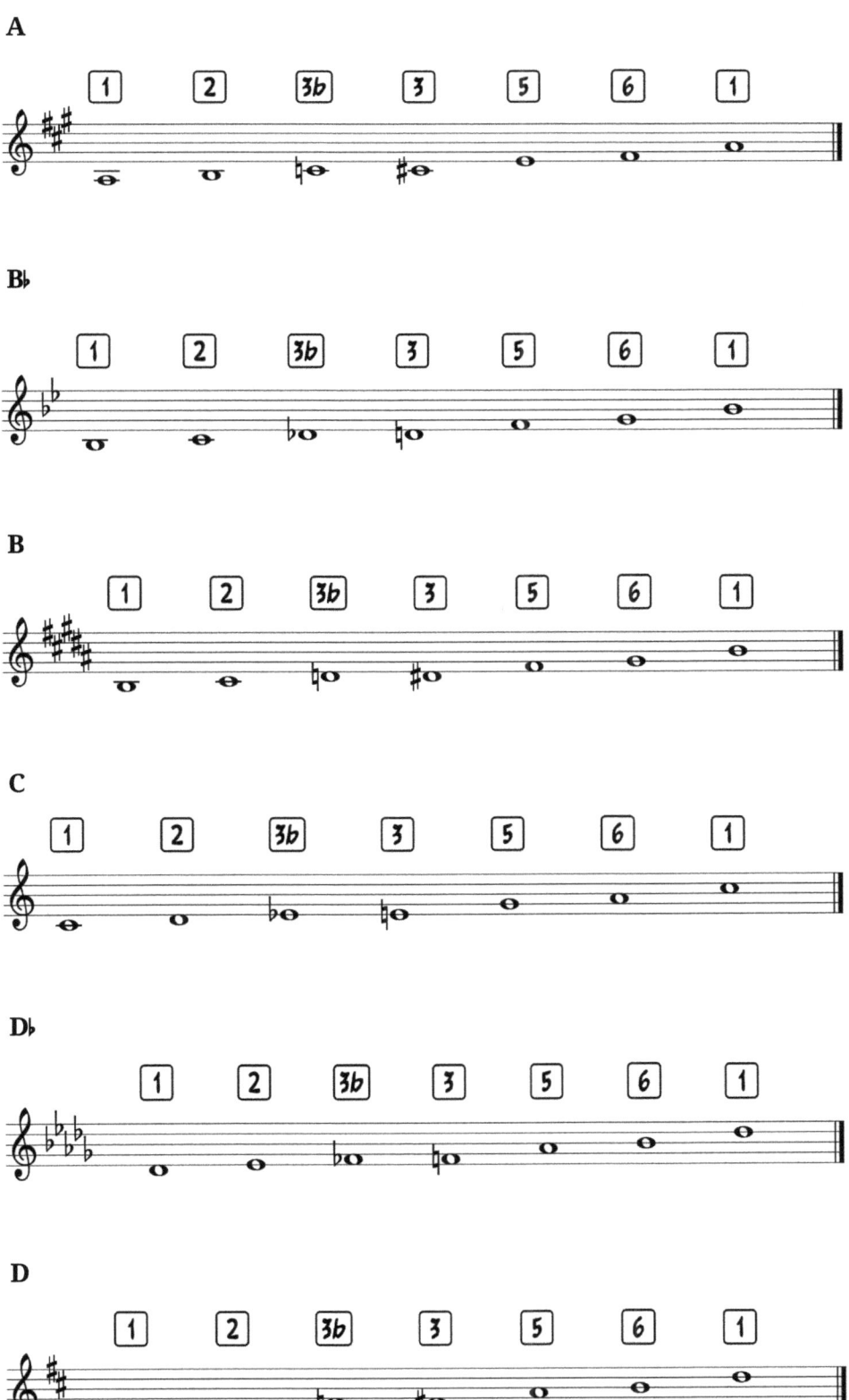

Major-Blues Scales

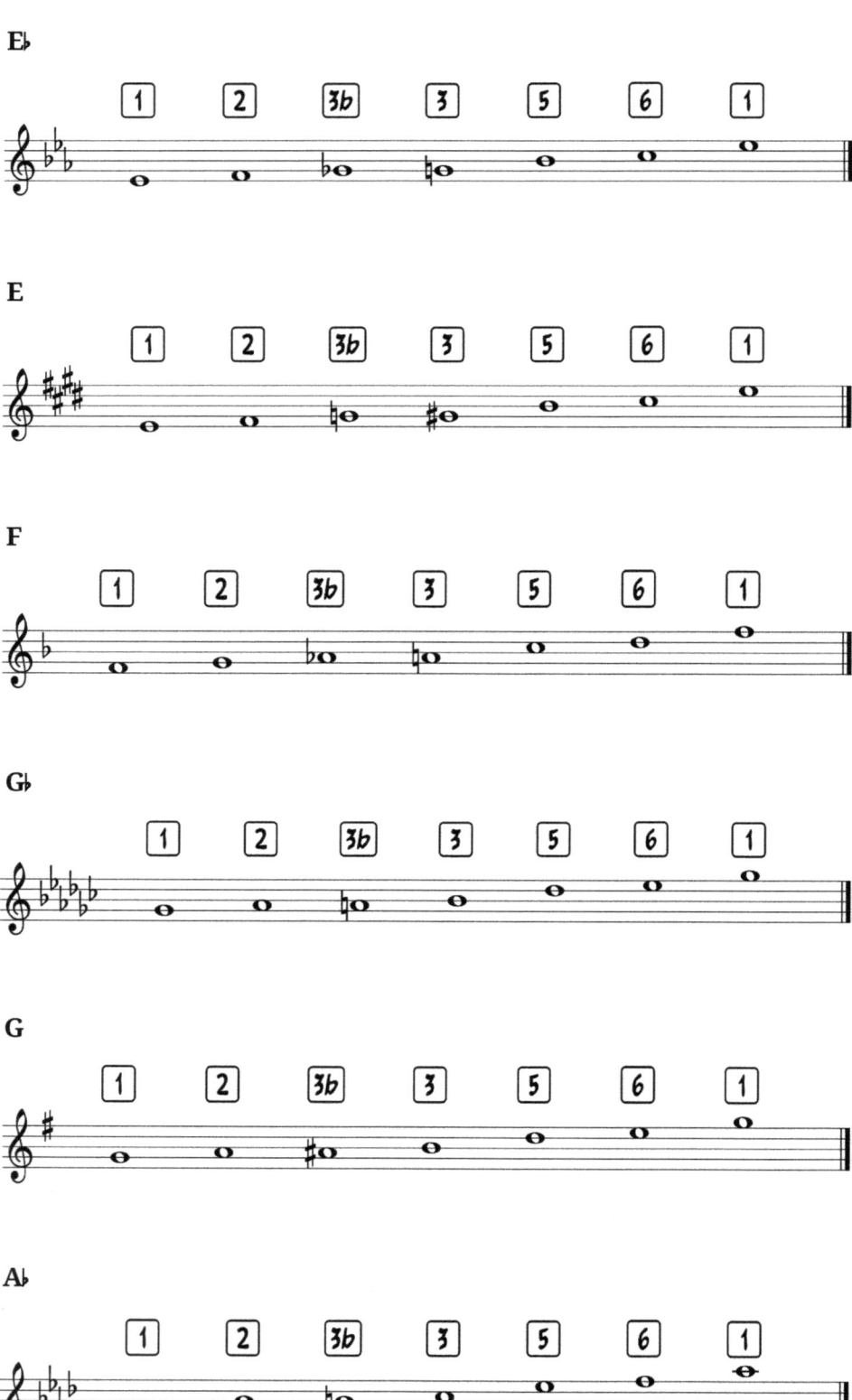

Minor-Blues Scales

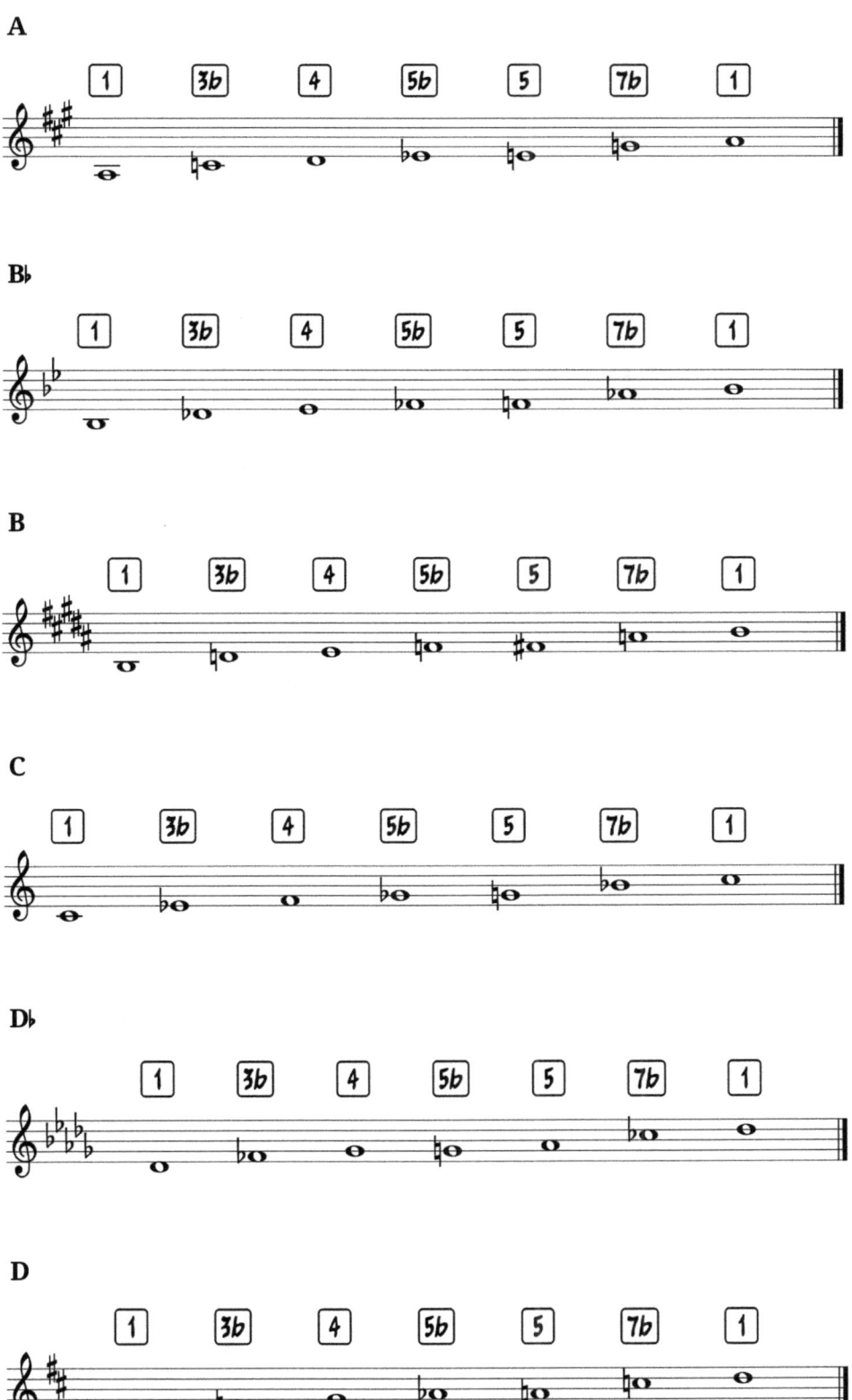

Minor-Blues Scales

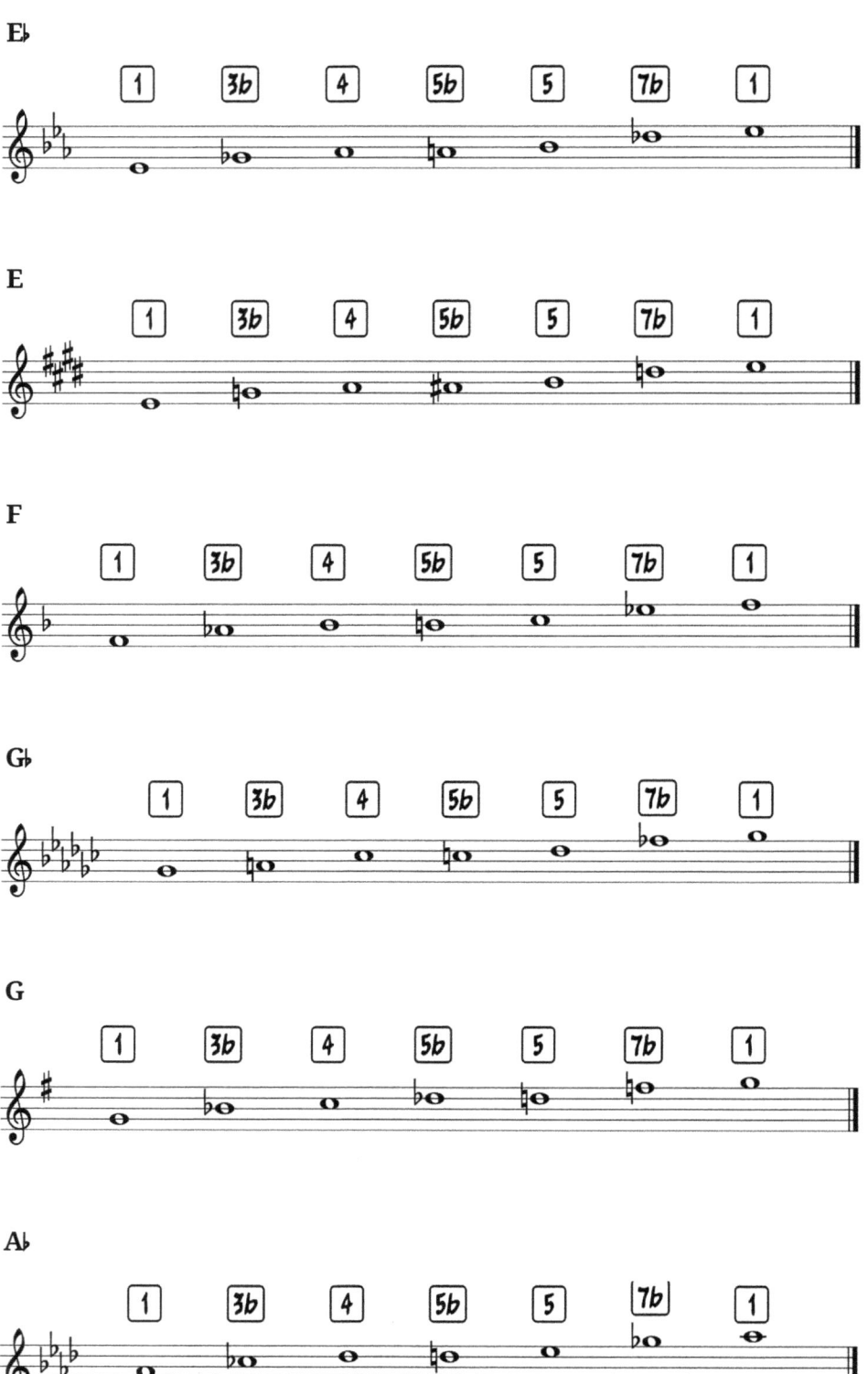

Relative Minors

Just as with the regular major-scales, the major pentatonic/major blues scales have relative minors (the minor pentatonic/minor blues scales). A relative minor scale uses exactly the same notes as the major scale it relates to, but with a different root note.

The sixth degree of the major scale dictates its relative minor. The sixth degree of 'C' major is a 'A', therefore the relative minor of 'C' major-blues is 'A' minor-blues.

'C' Major Blues Scale

'A' Minor Blues Scale

You can see above how these two related scales use the same notes. Now while knowing the relative minor relationship doesn't make a great deal of difference to your playing, knowledge of what you are dealing with always helps. One benefit is that once you know the notes to one scale, you actually also know them for its relative scale.

It's important to differentiate the major from the minor blues scale. Although the notes of 'A-minor blues' are the same as 'C-major blues' you're not playing 'A-minor blues' over that 'C' chord, it's 'C-major blues'.

Making this distinction is important, always consider them separate whilst practicing, it will help no end, not to mention being the correct way of thinking.

How To Practice

Getting started practising these scales is simple enough, although I'm not going to include endless and endless pages of scales here, but we will have a few suggestions on how you might practise them.

You will notice that I'm not including the left-hand here. Although it's normal practice to go over scales using both hands on the piano, in boogie-woogie this isn't really an efficient use of your time. The left-hand is generally (ninety-nine percent of the time) doing its own thing, normally a repetitive rhythmic pattern that will not benefit from endless practising of scales. The right-hand of course is different, and knowing these scales is very important. By all means, feel free to practise them with the left-hand too, it's just that it won't benefit you so much for this particular style.

Practice Over One Octave

Practice Over Two Octaves

Practice Over Three Octaves

Major

Minor

If a scale is new to you, then I would start by just practising over a single octave, run up the scale and then run down repeatedly. This is probably the best way to initially get the scale into your head. Once you are happy with it, you can practice over longer distances, two or three octaves worth perhaps, and from there even divide the scale up into patterns.

Different Keys

Naturally not everything is in the key of '**C**', so you will need to learn these in various keys. You can either try and learn them all at the same time, or just choose the ones that correspond to the particular keys you are concentrating on at the moment. Don't feel that you should practise it everything at once and know it instantly, take your time and go at your own speed.

Pentatonic Scales

The pentatonic scales are in essence the basis of the blues scales. Although they are important to know generally, I wouldn't necessarily over practice them for boogie-woogie use, but rather be aware that you can omit that single note and be within them. That's just a suggestion to save time, feel free to practise them separately if you wish.

The Scales Within

As an example of how the blues scales create the riffs and patterns in boogie-woogie piano, we are going to highlight a few sections of the next exercise piece to show how they consist (at least partly) of these scales. I'd skip ahead and take a quick look of the example first perhaps and then come back here. It's quite simple, but think about how some notes are from within the blues scales as you play, and the different intervals used.

Take the first bar, you will find that it consists entirely of notes from the major-blues scale.

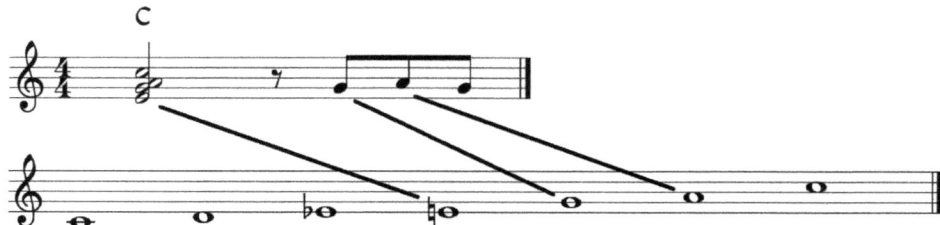

Or here on the '**IV**' chord, it is created predominantly from the '**F**' major-blues scale (with the exception of E-flat), which is found in the minor-blues scale.

In case you are wondering how the E-natural fits in here (as it isn't found in either the major or minor blues scale of the '**F**' chord) it does so in two ways.

The E-note can be found within the '**C**' major-blues scale and seeing as that is the '**I**' chord in this key, it will work over all the chords, '**I**', '**IV**' and '**V**'.

The E-note also works as it comes from the following chord of the next bar, so it leads into it. This is a common thing and can be heard being done quite often.

Scales Within One

Scales Within Two

The following is another example of how the music is formed from the blues scales. Using a variation of a commonly used riff, we can see how it is based around both of the blues scales. Again it is quite easy, but think about how some notes come from within the blues scales as you play and the different intervals used.

Major-Blues Scale

You can see how every note but one, is found in the major blues scale. The exception being the B-flat.

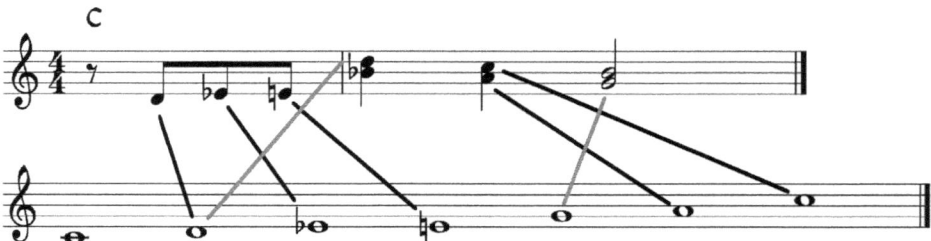

Minor-Blues Scale

Here you can see that the B-flat used that was missing from the major-blues scale can be found within the minor-blues scale, along with a few others as well.

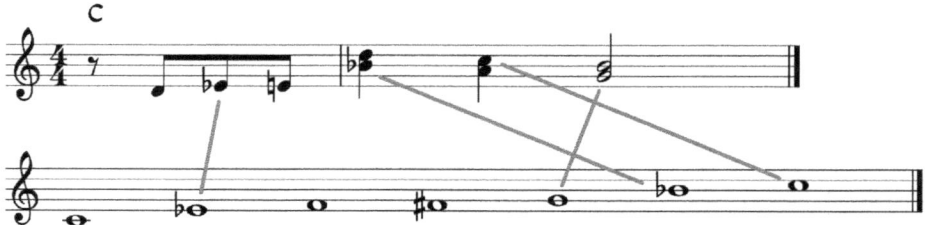

The scales work either singularly or when combined. When used in combination there are only three notes left that aren't available (or at least need extreme care).

- Flat-ninth
- Flat-sixth
- Major-seventh

Scales Within Two

Which Scale?

Knowing some scales is one thing, actually doing something constructive with them is something else. The aim of the game with boogie-woogie should be to learn how to improvise. You do this by learning a selection of riffs, creating a palette of possibilities that you can drop into when you feel fit, but you also do this by tapping into the notes from the scales that suit the music.

For the most part here we are going to be playing around using single note lines (as in only using a single note at a time) as opposed to more complex stuff. Call them twiddly bits if you like (it's how I refer to this kind of boogie stuff anyway, not exactly a technical term, but it fits).

What Scale To Use

What am I talking about here? Well this is the strange thing about blues music which you may well know. Whatever key you are playing in, the blues scales of that key will work over all three chords of a twelve-bar blues. This goes against traditional music theory and so in theory it shouldn't work, but nobody told the original blues masters this, so it definitely does work, it's all part of the magic.

You can of course also use the scales from the individual chords that you are on also. So in the key of '**C**' you could use the '**C**' blues scales over all three chords, or use the scales from that specific chord. The chart below shows which scales are useable over which chords.

Scale Usable Over Chords

Chord	Usable Scale
I	I
IV	I or IV
V	I or V

Options For scales Over Chords

Key	I Chord	IV Chord	V Chord
A	A	A or D	A or E
B♭	B♭	B♭ or E♭	B♭ or F
B	B	B or E	B or G♭
C	C	C or F	C or G
D♭	D♭	D♭ or G♭	D♭ or A♭
D	D	D or G	D or A
E♭	E♭	E♭ or A♭	E♭ or B♭
E	E	E or A	E or B
F	F	F or B♭	F or C
G♭	G♭	G♭ or B	G♭ or D♭
G	G	G or C	G or D
A♭	A♭	A♭ or D♭	A♭ or E♭

Which Ones To Use?

So you have your options, but which ones are best to use? (Bear in mind, here we are only talking about single note twiddly bits, not more complex patterns made up of intervals and chords). So generally speaking you can't go wrong using the base 'I' key as this always sounds great, it's perhaps what's used more than anything else. The way the 'I' chord scales work over all the chords is a big part of the blues sound. The 'IV' and 'V' scales can of course be used over their matching chords, but can be a little trickier to fit in well. It's possible to transpose the same pattern used on the 'I' chord to the other chords, as there aren't any rules as such, nobody has written a rule book that must be obeyed, so learn the scales and experiment. What is learnt in this manner goes deeper than that which you are taught.

> The following page has examples of how the scales sound over the chords. The first uses the 'I' chords scale over all three chords, the other uses the scale matching each of the individual chords.

The 'I' Minor-Blues Scale Over All Chords

Matching Minor-Blues Scale Over Each Chord

Twiddly Boogie Riffs

Knowledge of scales helps in general playing/improvising regardless of what you are doing, but the easiest or best place to start is with single note twiddly riffs. Keeping with a single note pattern is less to think about to begin with, plus it's very fairly common thing for the right-hand anyway.

Improvising isn't magic, and certainly in the simple form we are doing here (single notes). We are taking a set of notes (from a scale or two) and rearranging them into a different order that will hopefully sound musical.

There are different ways you could approach beginning this, but we are going to try to split it up into different ideas, the first of which is splitting the scale into groupings. This is just a case of only using a number of the notes from the scale at a time (say three or maybe four) and creating a repeating pattern from them only. You might then move to a different position within the scale and use a different set of notes. Ultimately you won't think in these terms once you are more practised, but it's a good way to set limits in order to make it easier to do something that's new to you.

We are going to split the scales up into three, four and five note groupings, which within each you can come up with various combinations of notes with different timings/rhythmic ideas. Doing this in stages like this will help you get comfortable with the scales, getting the physical patterns committed to your muscle memory and easier to recall. The more notes in the group, the more complex the possibilities are, gradually increasing until you use all/any available notes to improvise with and are completely free. But remember that the simple smaller patterns that use just a few notes are always used, sometimes less is definitely more.

Minor Blues Scale

Three Note Grouping Ideas

Here the minor-blues scale has been split and grouped into only three notes. This is commonly used in a triplet form as shown here. The twelve-bar example is just for practice purposes, you wouldn't want to repeat the same pattern for this long in reality.

Practice Twelve-Bar Example

Four Note Grouping Examples

Three notes is fine at times but a little limiting, so now we will step it up to four notes. Below are a few examples of patterns created using the minor-blues scale. Again, this is only a tiny sample of the possibilities.

Practice Twelve-Bar Example

A short example of some patterns built around four note groupings using the minor-blues scale.

Experiment yourself by improvising patterns using four note groupings over a twelve-bar. Sticking to only four notes is a little limiting, but it's good practice. Feel free to try it in as many keys as you wish.

Improvise Over Twelve-Bars

Five Note Grouping Examples

Here we have some examples that are using five notes from the minor-blues scale.

Practice Twelve Bar Example

A short example of some patterns built around five note groupings using the minor-blues scale.

Experiment yourself by improvising patterns using five note groupings over a twelve-bar. Sticking to five notes is still limiting ultimately, but it's good practice. Feel free to try it in as many keys as you wish.

Improvise Over Twelve-Bars

Minor-Blues Patterns

The examples below allow for the use of all the notes within the minor-blues scale.

Major Blues Groupings

Don't neglect the major-blues scale as it is an important aspect of boogie-woogie playing, so with that in mind let's run over the same idea with the major-blues scale.

Three Note Grouping Ideas

These are all created from the same major-blues scale, merely different combinations of notes in different orders.

Practice Twelve-Bar Example

Four Note Grouping Examples

Here we have a few examples of four note groupings created from the major-blues scale.

Practice Twelve-Bar Example

A short example of some patterns built around four note groupings using the major-blues scale.

Experiment yourself by improvising patterns using four note groupings over a twelve-bar. Remember not to limit yourself to just one key.

Improvise Over Twelve-Bars

Five Note Grouping Examples

Here we have some examples that are using five notes from the major-blues scale.

Practice Twelve-Bar Example

A short twelve-bar example using some patterns built around five note groupings from the major-blues scale.

Experiment yourself by improvising patterns using five note groupings over a twelve-bar. Feel free to try it in as many keys as you wish.

Improvise Over Twelve-Bars

Full Major-Blues Patterns

The examples below allow for the full use of all the notes within the major-blues scale.

Notes On Following Song Examples

The next two song examples incorporate a lot of single note twiddly bits like we have been looking at, but they differ in a couple of ways.

The first one primarily plays around within the minor-blues scale, while the second is mostly the major-blues scales (with the odd exceptions in places). You should be able to hear the difference in the sound they create, even though they are in different keys.

The other difference is that the second song goes further and also incorporates chords rather than being singular notes throughout, and it does this in two ways.

1.

Using chords within actual riffs built from chords rather than only using single notes.

2.

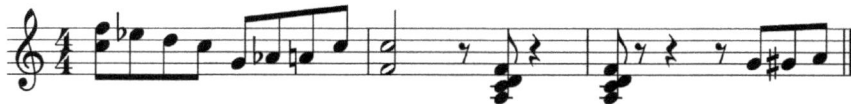

Switching between twiddly single note sections and rhythmic chord parts. This could be like above, where the change is frequent, switching every couple of bars. Or you could have twelve bars of twiddly patterns and then twelve bars of rhythmic chord parts before going back to twiddly stuff again.

Play through the song examples but as you do, think about what the notes are, or rather where they came from, how they fit within the scales we have looked at. When you are done, perhaps play around with them, alter parts or create new parts along the same lines that would fit with the existing music.

Twiddly Boogie Minor

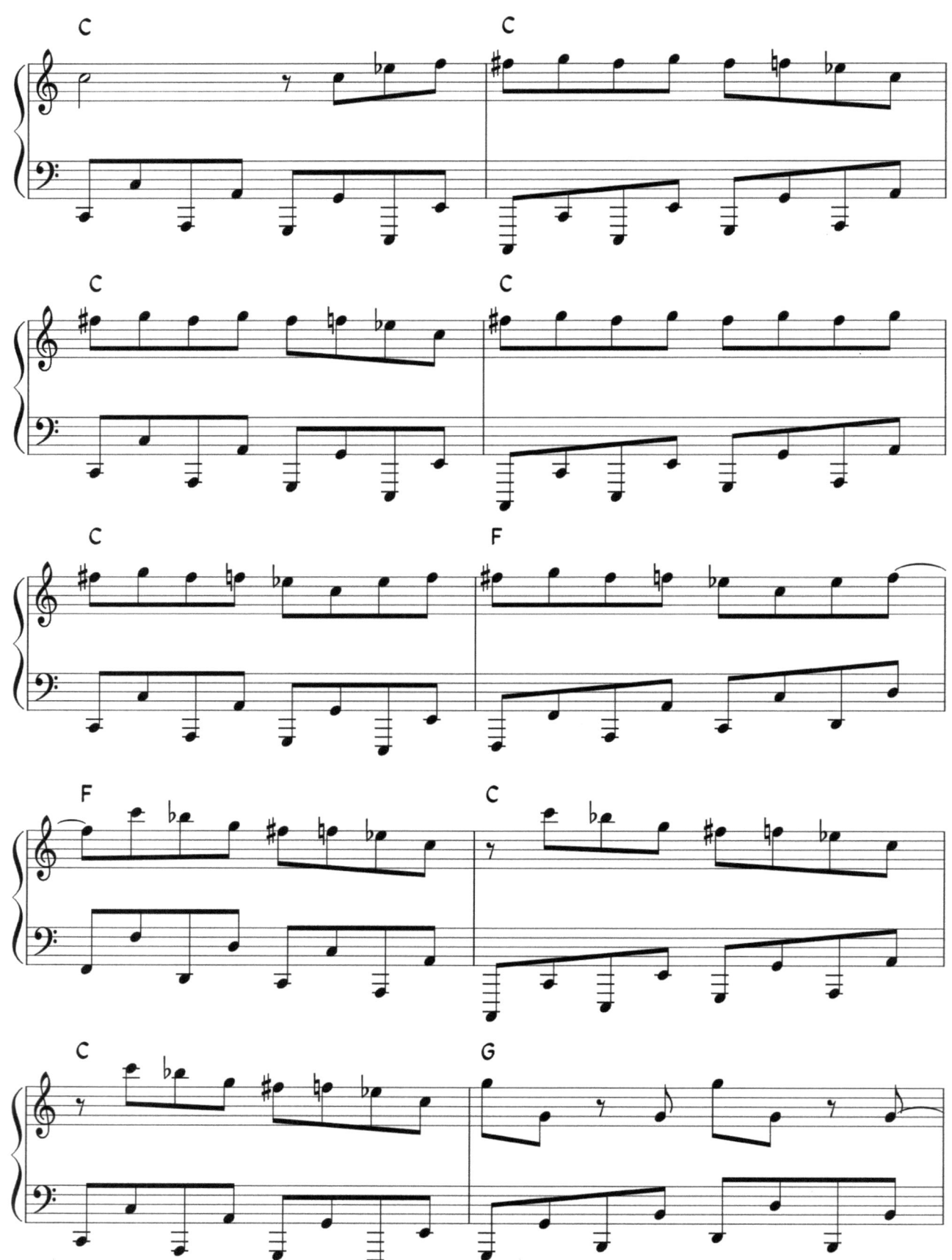

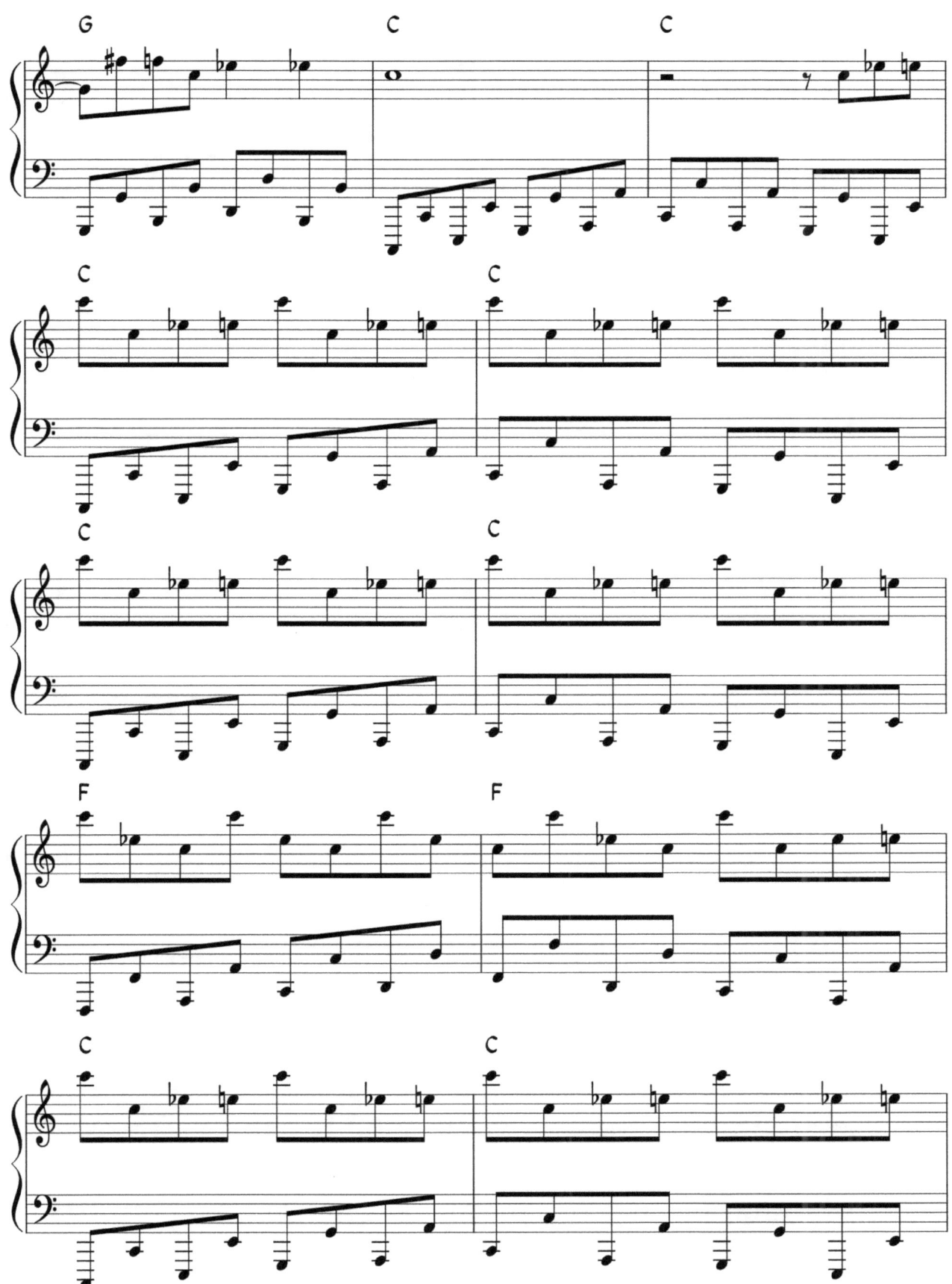

Twiddly Boogie Major

Creating Twiddly Riffs

We've looked at the scales commonly used along with some example riffs, we've also had a couple of song examples based mainly on either minor or major scales. If this is new to you then hopefully it will have given you some ideas for improvising. Admittedly it's hardly exhaustive as there are many styles of play and far more riffs and ideas than can be fitted into any book, but it's a start.

Between both the minor and major blues scales we actually have the majority of the notes available to us.

Combined Blues Scales In 'C'

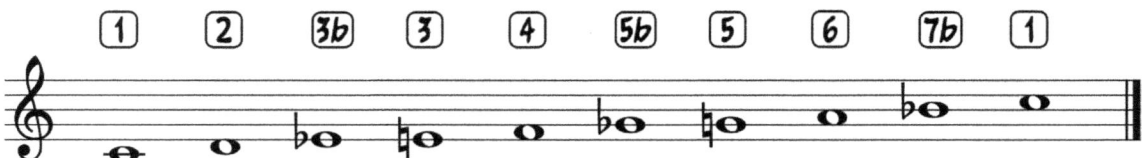

You may notice that there aren't that many of the notes missing, only three to be exact.

Missing Notes

This isn't to say that the two scales combine well necessarily, they do and they don't. If you play around with the combination above you'll find that some combination of notes work okay, others sound quite rough, experimentation is the best way to learn. An easier way to begin to combine the two is to use them separately, but to flow from one to another.

Some Possible Options

1. Start in major-blues and swap to minor
2. Start with minor-blues and end in major
3. Start in major, swap to minor and back to major
4. Start in minor, swap to major and then back to minor
5. Start with a blues scale and end with a pentatonic
6. Start within a pentatonic scale and end in a blues scale

Major To Minor

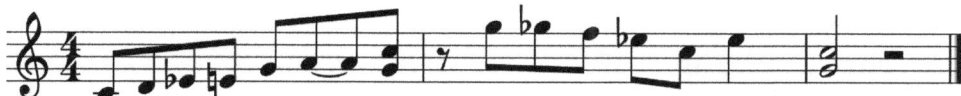

Minor To Major

Major To Minor And Back To Major

Minor To Major And Back To Minor

Blues Scale To Pentatonic

Pentatonic To Blues Scale

New From Old

If you are new to improvising then the best advice I can give is to just have a go, play something, play anything, but play something. We have looked at some of the tools that you can use, so it's a matter of getting stuck in and seeing what you come up with. It's just a matter of time, patients and of course lots of practice.

The simplest place to start is perhaps taking an existing pattern or riff and play around with it, altering it into something new. Below is what may be a familiar pattern.

Initial Pattern One

Now you could take this and alter it in many ways. Changing parts, shortening it, lengthening it, repeating sections. Next we'll look at some examples of what we could potentially do with this pattern to alter it.

Example. 1

Here we've taken the very first part and disregarded the rest, creating something new from what we already have.

Example. 2

We could make slight alterations to this to change it further. Here we have simply repeated the last notes.

Example. 3

This adds a little to the second half/repeat. It still uses the same notes as the original pattern, they're just rearranged.

Example. 4

Here the second bar moves more like the original, but instead of continuing downwards it moves back up.

Example. 5

The last bar is closer to the original, but ends higher with the tied notes of longer duration.

Example. 6

Here we change the timing/feel by switching to using triplets.

Example. 7

Now we have changed the initial three notes into triplets, which also moves them along the timeline.

Example. 8

Moving back towards the original, instead of repeating, it continues in a downward direction.

Example. 9

A slight variation that uses the flat-third and flat-fifth.

Example. 10

Here it moves down further, still using mostly thirds.

Example. 11

Losing the flat-fifth this time, the last bar repeats the same pattern of the flat-third moving to the third. It is also busier than previously as it doesn't have the rest at the end.

Example. 12

This time the second bar moves up to include the flat-seventh and also ends higher with the fifth and root.

Here we have another pattern to play around with and create something new. This time it's using only single notes.

Initial Pattern Two

Now we can look at ways to make something new out of the source material, using the same ideas, removing parts, repeating parts and adding something new here and there.

Example. 1

First we have taken the pattern and removed a lot of it, keeping the first five notes and then repeating them again, the extra end note gives it some finality.

Example. 2

Here we have taken the first example and added an ending that is similar in fashion to the original.

Example. 3

Now we have added an extra fill note to the second bar with a variation of example two on the end.

Example. 4

This time it has been shortened considerably by removing the whole of the last bar.

Example. 5

Here we have repeated the triplet part, playing it again in the third bar with a few extra notes to finish.

Example. 6

This time we have made even more of the triplet pattern and repeated it right across the two bars.

Example. 7

Here we use the double triplet part but then revert to the same last bar as the original pattern.

Example. 8

Now we have removed the triplets but retained the notes from the triplet part (changing the timing). The last bar is simply a repeat of the second bar.

Example. 9

Now we have taken it in a slightly different direction. Starting off the same but then using the flat-seventh to create a new pattern that's repeated a couple of times.

Example. 10

This has similarities to the original, using some of the same notes minus the triplet timing and with a longer note to end.

Example. 11

Here we have taken the first five notes and then repeated them three times, moving up an octave each time with just a slight rest in-between.

Example. 12

This time we take the previous example but instead of repeating the pattern a third time an octave higher, we give it a simple ending instead.

Altering/changing/playing around with existing patterns/riffs is a good way to create something new. Ultimately we learn by copying from what has been done before, so don't feel that you should be creating new material from thin air by magic, as it really doesn't work like that. When improvising you are drawing upon all the information that you have assimilated and can instantly recall for use. This will be built up of a lot of music that you have learnt from existing material, so using such material to work from is a fine way to develop skills.

Example Patterns To Practice With

Here's a few riffs/patterns to practice creating new things from. I won't include too many here as you can use any boogie-woogie sheet music you have, or alternatively do the same from recorded music if you can learn/play by ear. This is something I would encourage you to learn to do.

Example. 1

Example. 2

Example. 3

Example. 4

Example. 5

Example. 6

Example. 7

Example. 8

Example. 9

Example. 10

See what you can create from these, but then take the idea much further and play around with other music that you have. It's a good way to get started improvising as you have a base to work from.

Listen To Music

Listen To The Music

To take your improvising skills further, by far the best thing to do is to listen to boogie-woogie music. Learn as much as you can from sheet music as well, but it's really important to listen to as much recorded boogie-woogie material as you can, as often as possible. This will internalise the sound you are after, and I can't stress enough how essential it is.

Why Does This Help

When you listen to a lot of music, your brain gets used to how that sounds on a subconscious level. This is useful as once you have learnt the basic rules of what the music is made up off – scales/chords – then you have the tools or information to be able to re-create what you hear on the piano. This should result in a gradual process whereas you improvise, you will naturally re-create some of what you have listened to. I'm not talking about an exact copy necessarily (although that's good) but that internalised sound of the music will find its way to your keyboard as you play and re-create that music.

Patients

Bear in mind that this isn't a quick fix, it's a slow, long-drawn-out process, that won't happen overnight. But if you listen to anyone who has reached a good level of proficiency, then you have someone that has most likely listened and copied. Plus, there's a near unlimited amount of resources (recorded music) to learn from, as opposed to the relatively limited amount of sheet music available. Also, you can learn anything you hear without needing the sheet music for it, which may or may not be available, more likely not in reality. The classic songs are available for sure but anything more modern or obscure you probably won't find available.

Changing Position

If you have a riff that you play in one position on the keyboard, it can sometimes get repetitive if it's played too often. A way around this and to create a little more interest is to repeat the same thing but to move it up (or down) an octave or two. It's still the same pattern of notes, but by changing the position on the keyboard (and so the pitch) it does sound a little different.

Take the little pattern below as an example.

You could repeat this exactly as it is several times in a row, or instead you could switch the position of it each time. One idea isn't better than the other, it's simply another option.

Repeated Once (One Octave Apart)

Repeated Twice (Each One Octave Apart)

Altered Version

You could also repeat the pattern as before, moving up the keyboard an octave at a time and then bring it to a conclusion.

Repeating riff type patterns at different positions is one option, you can also switch octaves while playing more rhythmic chord based parts. It's the same chord (possibly a different inversion if you wish) but moving it an octave or two will make it sound a little different.

Twelve-Bar Example

The next song example employs this idea of jumping around the keyboard. Playing parts in different octave ranges can make the music more interesting, both to listen to and to play. You have a nice long keyboard, so make use of it.

Different Ideas/Options

1.

A 'twiddly' part above, and then moving down for a few chords. You can always move back up again afterward.

2.

Playing chords at different ranges.

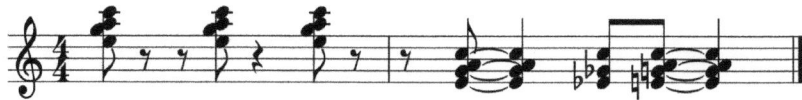

3.

Playing/repeating the same pattern at different ranges.

The example piece also takes a few liberties with the blues twelve-bar chord progression in a couple of places.

- Replacing the '**V**' and '**IV**' chords on bars 9/10 with a '**II**' and '**V**'.

- Replacing '**V**' and '**IV**' chords on bars 9/10 with two '**V**' chords.

- Adding two extra bars at the beginning of a twelve-bar section (two extra '**I**' chords). Although the basic progressions tends to be adhered to, you can take liberties and add additional bars.

Switch The Boogie

117

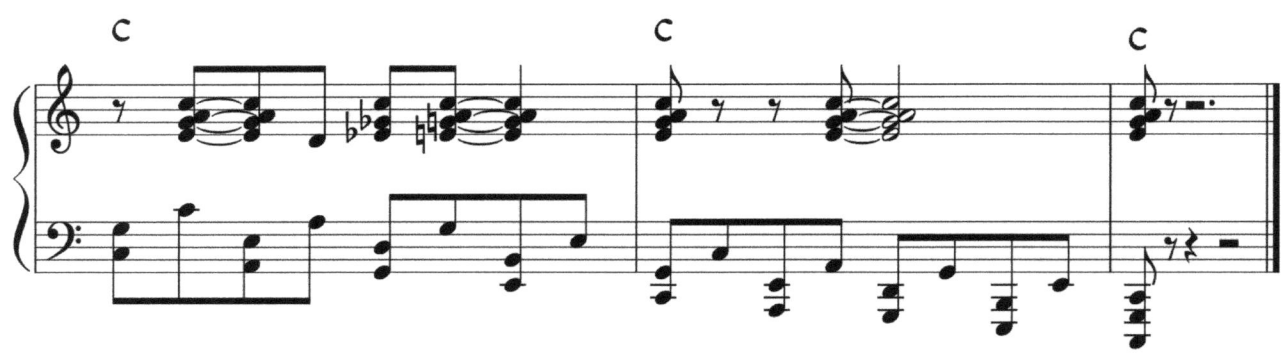

16-Bar Progression

There are other chord progressions that you can use if you wish, so we will take a quick look at some options, starting with the sixteen-bar variety. None of these are as common as the twelve, but they're well worth knowing, and you might have fun playing in a different format.

16-Bar Chord Progression Example

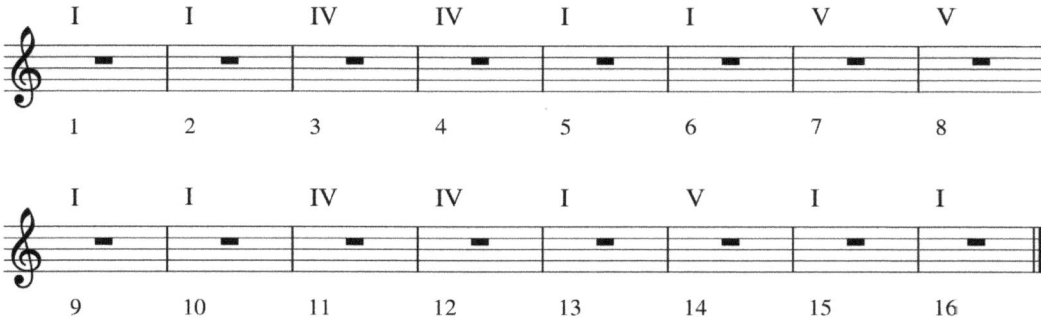

You can see how it jumps to the 'V' chord more often than in a twelve-bar progression. Also notice that unlike the twelve-bar progression it doesn't have the 'V' and 'IV' chords together. It sounds a little different of course and feels different to play, plus it makes a nice change from the usual endless twelve-bars we so typically play.

This can be modified further by adding another (altered) sixteen-bars on to the end of it, creating in essence a thirty-two bar chord progression.

32-Bar Chord Progression Example

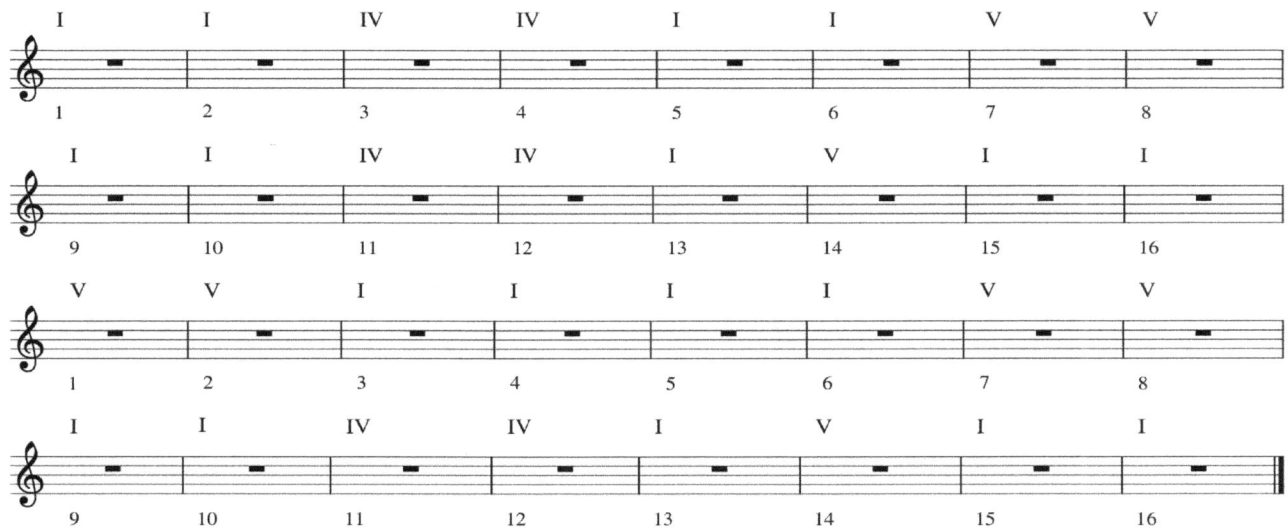

Sixteen Boogie

Thirty-Two Boogie

24-Bar Boogie

Here we have another option that you can play around with. Although the twelve-bar format is the common way of doing things, and we have sixteen bars/thirty-two bars, we also can use a twenty-four bar chord progression.

24-Bar Chord Progression

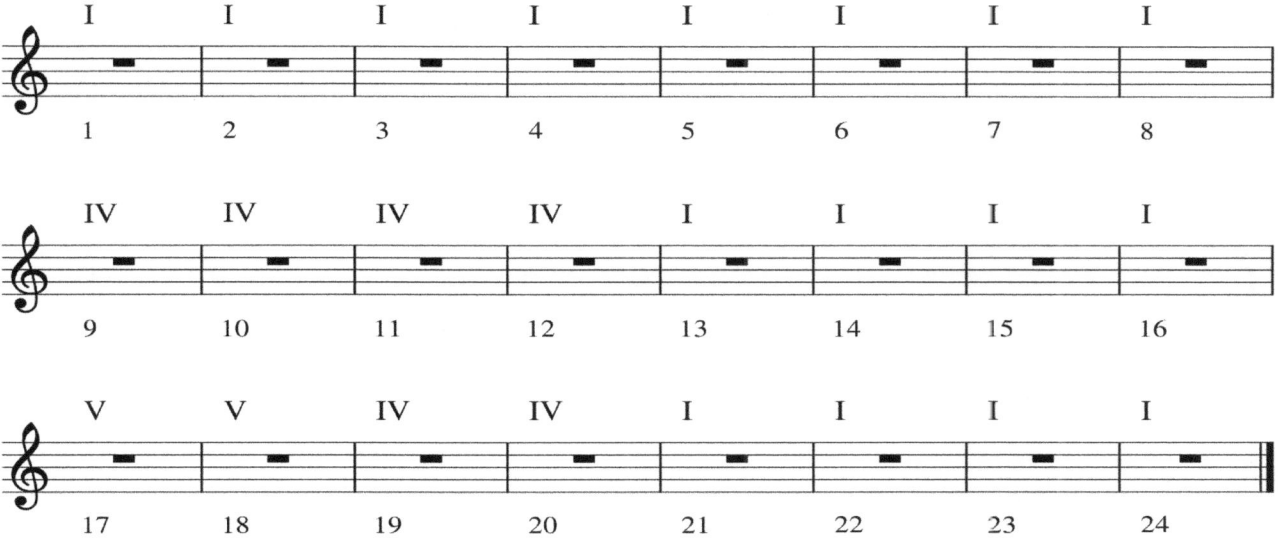

Unlike the sixteen and thirty-two bar chord progression we looked at previously, this isn't so different to the twelve-bar, in-fact it is largely the same. The difference is that it doubles up on all the chords to stretch it out to twice the length. Instead of starting with four bars of the '**I**' chord, we have eight. Instead of following with two bars of the '**IV**' chord, we have four, and so it continues throughout.

It isn't slower as such, but it does give you more time to play with. More time to develop an idea within each chord or section of the progression. In a sense it's more relaxed, in that you have more time to think, but again, that will depend on what you actually are playing.

Twenty-Four Boogie

Practicing Suggestions

It's pretty obvious that the more time you spend practicing the better you will get, but how much time you spend will be very personal to you, as different peoples spare time will vary a lot. But I will say one thing, consistency is the key.

CONSISTENCY

CONSISTENCY

CONSISTENCY

Yes, in-case I haven't made myself clear, being consistent is quite helpful. It's really helpful in-fact and will make a huge difference to your progression compared to an inconsistent, on and off, practice one week and miss a week kind of affair.

The best way to progress is to practice every day, this would keep the music fresh in your mind. The constant drilling/repetition on a daily basis is how we force the brain to remember and so learn new things. When I say every day, don't panic, it doesn't necessarily mean hours and hours (although if you can, great) but whatever time you can spare. Even ten minutes helps if that's all you have, the main thing is to keep it regular without large gaps in-between. Little and often, is usually far more effective than cramming lots of practice in on just one day and then doing nothing for a week.

Metronome

Using a metronome whilst practicing is highly recommended. The use of one will really help with keeping the timing tight throughout and stop the tempo from drifting too much (although a little is perfectly normal, we aren't machines after-all). When I say metronome, use whatever you have which might be a mechanical metronome, a digital one, even an app on your phone. Playing along to a drum backing is also an option, and sometimes it's even preferable for polishing something you can play, as it adds something to the music and makes it more exciting/interesting and enjoyable.

Downloadable Audio

Audio files based on the examples within the book are available to download from the website in MP3 format, simply follow the instructions below.

To access and download the MP3 audio files, simply visit the website...

www.tylermusic.co.uk

- Click on audio downloads
- Select the relevant book title
- Enter the password... **vol3improvising822**

Once downloaded please save them for future use or simply bookmark the website download page.

Tyler music.co.uk

For further piano books (including spiral bound editions)
sheet music and information on blues
and boogie woogie music
visit the website at…

www.tylermusic.co.uk

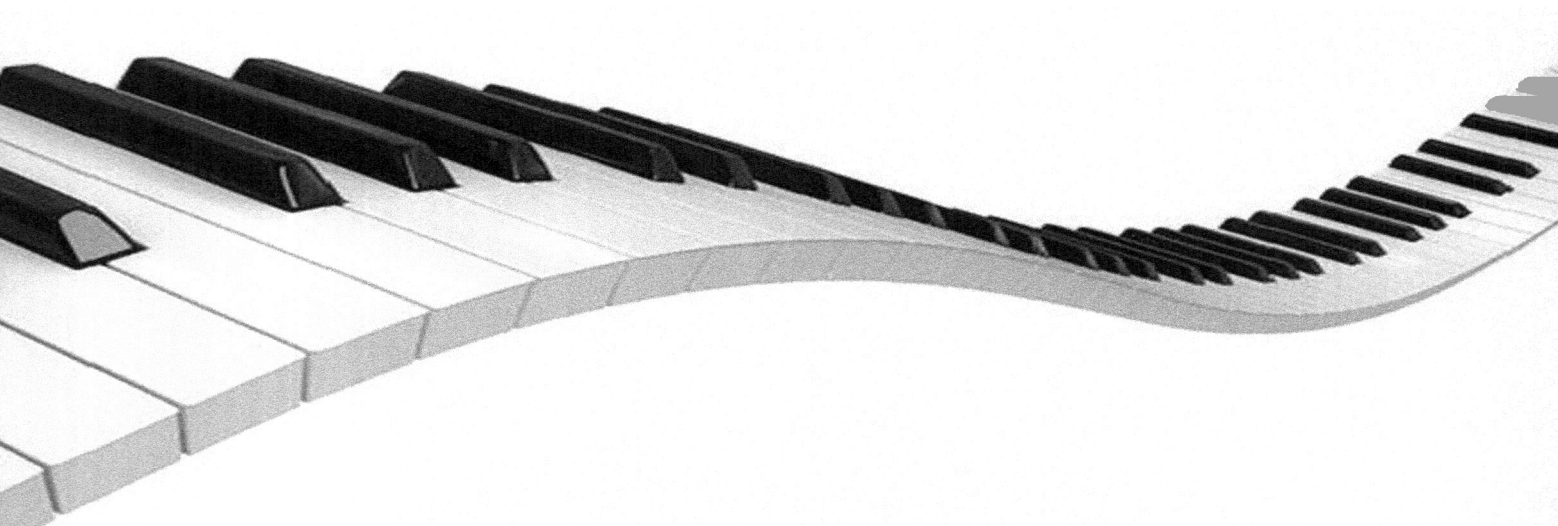

**Follow us on Facebook for updates
and information on latest releases.**

Also Available

Improvising Boogie-Woogie Vol. One & Two

Learn to play boogie-woogie like the best of them. If you want to play boogie like Albert Ammons, Axel Zwingenberger or Jools Holland then this is the series for you. The first volume in a series of books to teach boogie-woogie piano, from the basics to more advanced techniques and everything in-between, this will give you the help and material you need.

Improvising Boogie-Woogie: The Complete Edition

All three volumes in one edition. Available as perfect bound and spiral bound (spiral available through the website only). Learn to play boogie-woogie like the best of them. If you want to play boogie like Albert Ammons, Axel Zwingenberger or Jools Holland then this is the series for you. From the basics to more advanced techniques and everything in-between.

Easy Boogie-Woogie   For Beginners

Easy boogie-woogie takes the beginning boogie pianist through their first steps into the timeless style. It covers the basics with easy to understand clear explanations and includes example pieces throughout that start off easy and gradually increase in difficulty while adding extra elements. With downloadable audio, why not start learning boogie-woogie today.

Easy Boogie-Woogie Vol.2

This second volume of Easy Boogie-Woogie follows on from the first one, taking the beginning boogie player a step further again. New ideas and concepts are introduced along with many examples and explanations throughout. Bigger and better than ever. With downloadable audio to help you along, it's the perfect way to continue your boogie-woogie journey.

Easy Blues Piano   For Beginners

Learn to play the blues with this beginners guide for the piano. It covers the very basics of the blues, introducing the various elements that create the twelve-bar blues sound. It starts off easy, so even a relative beginner can dive in, and gradually introduces new ideas. With downloadable audio, why not start learning blues today.

Easy New-Orleans   For Beginners

Learn to play that unique style of blues piano from New Orleans, the style of Dr John, Professor Longhair and James Booker to name but a few. Covering everything from chord progressions and left-hand bass patterns and introducing the all important New-Orleans rhythm.

Easy Rock 'N' Roll   For Beginners

Easy rock 'n' roll is for the beginner taking their first steps into the timeless sound of rock 'n' roll piano. Covering the basics with easy to understand clear explanations on how to play in the style of the likes of Jerry Lee Lewis and Little Richard. It includes example pieces throughout that start off easy and gradually increase in difficulty, while adding extra elements along the way. With downloadable audio

The Complete Blues Piano

The complete blues piano is a comprehensive guide to playing and improvising blues piano. It covers the fundamental principles of the blues and includes in-depth theory and techniques, along with example blues pieces to learn/study with downloadable audio. Ranging from fast boogie-type blues to slow blues, Chicago through to New Orleans, beginners to intermediate, this has it covered.

Piano Blues Scales

The ultimate guide to learning the blues scales for the piano. The scales are clearly shown and explained in all keys for both major and minor scales along with fingering suggestions. But it doesn't stop there, here we go further and include ideas like the combined scales and methods of how to practice and use the scales in a more musical and practical real world fashion.

Bite Sized Specifics – Blues Piano/Walking-Bass

Learn to play the walking-bass for blues piano with the first in a series that concentrates on specific aspects of blues piano. Concentrating on the left-hand, it looks at what the walking-bass is, how it is created and various ways to which you can employ it in a blues environment.

Bite Sized Specifics – Blues Piano/Stride-Piano

Learn to play blues piano using the left-hand stride style. The second in a series that concentrates on a specific aspect of blues piano. Concentrating on the left-hand, it looks at what stride is and how it is created and various ways to which you can employ it in a blues environment.

Bite Sized Specifics – Blues Piano/Right-Hand Vol.1

Learn to play blues piano with the third in a series that concentrates on specific aspects of blues piano. Concentrating on the right-hand, it concentrates on the important aspect of comping, which is the more rhythmic side of blues with an emphasis on the important use of chords and repetitive patterns/riffs that form the backbone of the music.

Tyler Music – Blues & Boogie-Woogie Piano

www.ingramcontent.com/pod-product-compliance
Lightning Source LLC
Chambersburg PA
CBHW051315110526
44590CB00031B/4368